HOW TO BE A
DETECTIVE!

Crack the case with 25 devious disguises and devices!

Nick Huckleberry Beak

ARMADILLO

This edition is published by Armadillo, an imprint of Anness Publishing Ltd,
Blaby Road, Wigston, Leicestershire LE18 4SE; info@anness.com
www.annesspublishing.com

If you like the images in this book and would like to investigate using them for publishing, promotions
or advertising, please visit our website www.practicalpictures.com for more information.

Publisher: Joanna Lorenz
Managing Editor: Sue Grabham
Editors: Sam Batra, Lyn Coutts, Richard McGinlay
Photographer: John Freeman
Designer: Michael R Carter
Production Controller: Wendy Lawson

PUBLISHER'S NOTE
Although the advice and information in this book are believed to be accurate and true at the time of
going to press, neither the authors nor the publisher can accept any legal responsibility or liability
for any errors or omissions that may have been made nor for any inaccuracies nor for any loss,
harm or injury that comes about from following instructions or advice in this book.

Manufacturer: Anness Publishing Ltd, Blaby Road, Wigston, Leicestershire LE18 4SE, England
For Product Tracking go to: www.annesspublishing.com/tracking
Batch: 0670-22583-1127

Introduction

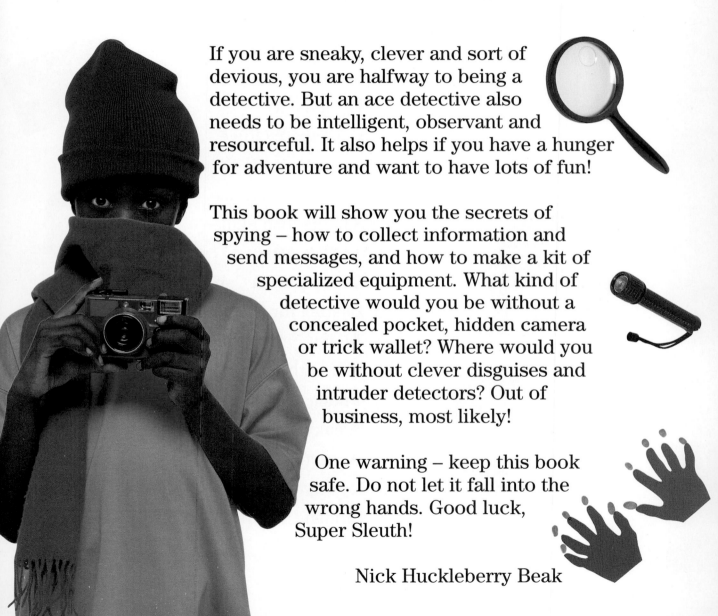

If you are sneaky, clever and sort of devious, you are halfway to being a detective. But an ace detective also needs to be intelligent, observant and resourceful. It also helps if you have a hunger for adventure and want to have lots of fun!

This book will show you the secrets of spying – how to collect information and send messages, and how to make a kit of specialized equipment. What kind of detective would you be without a concealed pocket, hidden camera or trick wallet? Where would you be without clever disguises and intruder detectors? Out of business, most likely!

One warning – keep this book safe. Do not let it fall into the wrong hands. Good luck, Super Sleuth!

Nick Huckleberry Beak

Contents

Materials

Thick book

Brown wrapping paper

Aluminium foil

Paper bag

Torch

Decks of playing cards

Mirrors

Lemon

ALUMINIUM FOIL
Use this material to complete an electrical circuit.

BATTERIES AND HOLDER
These items will be found at hardware and electrical stores. For the project in this book you will need two AA batteries.

BROWN WRAPPING PAPER
This can bought in sheets or rolls at stationery stores.

CARBON PAPER
One side of this paper is inky, the other is not. When placed inky side down, it makes a copy of whatever is written on the paper above.

CLEAR ADHESIVE PLASTIC
When the protective backing is peeled off, the clear plastic can be stuck to any surface. It can be bought at stationery stores.

CRUNCHY CEREAL
For the project in this book you will need a bowl of crispy flaked breakfast cereal. It must make a noise when stepped on.

DRINK CONTAINER
You can use either a plastic or disposable drink container.

FELT
Felt is a fabric that can be easily cut and does not fray. It comes in lots of bright shades.

INK PAD
A black ink pad is best for the project in this book. Always shut the lid on the ink pad after use to keep the pad moist.

MAGNIFYING GLASS
A glass, rather than plastic, lens makes it easier to see the fine detail in the enlarged image. Protect the lens from scratches by keeping it in a fabric pouch.

MIRRORS
You will need four small mirrors to make the projects in this book. The best ones are those mounted in a plastic frame with a plastic back.

PHOTOGRAPH OF YOURSELF
You will need a passport-size head-and-shoulders photo. Ask for permission before you cut up a family photograph!

PICTURE POSTCARD
For the project in this book, recycle an old postcard or cut the picture off a greetings card.

PLASTER OF PARIS
This is a white powder that sets hard when mixed with water. You can buy it at craft stores.

PLASTIC-COVERED ELECTRICAL WIRE
The fine strands of copper wire conduct electricity. This can be bought in rolls at electrical stores. Ask an adult to help you cut the wire.

Crunchy cereal

Mug

Small box

Talcum powder

Drink container

Plastic bowling pin

Camera

Photograph of yourself

Torch bulb and base

Carbon paper

Felt

Plaster of Paris

Batteries and holder

Envelopes

Plastic-covered electrical wire

Magnifying glass

Clear adhesive plastic

Squeakers

Confectionery in wrappers

Picture postcard

Ink pad

Notepad

POCKET CAMERA
You can use a pocket camera or buy a disposable one.

SQUEAKERS
These hollow plastic circles squeak when they are pressed. They are used in the making of stuffed toys and can be bought at haberdashery (notions) or craft stores.

TORCH (FLASHLIGHT)
For the projects in this book you only need a small, plastic torch. Do not forget to put in the batteries!

TORCH (FLASHLIGHT) BULB AND BASE
These can be bought at hardware and electrical stores. They are very inexpensive.

TALCUM POWDER
There is likely to be a container of this sweet-smelling powder in the bathroom in your home. Ask for permission before you borrow it.

THICK BOOK
Make sure the book you use is unwanted. If you cannot find one at home, buy one at a secondhand bookstore.

Equipment

Pencil sharpener

Needle and thread

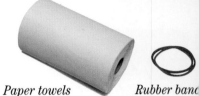

Paper towels

Rubber band

ADHESIVE TAPE
Clear or invisible tape is
needed for the projects
in this book.

BOWL
To make plaster of Paris, it is
best to use an old bowl. It is
sometimes hard to remove all
traces of dry plaster.

CARDBOARD AND PAPER
For the projects in this book
you will need sheets of plain
white paper and sheets of
cardboard in various shades.
You can use either thin or
stiff cardboard.

ELECTRICAL TAPE
This is a very strong tape that is
available in lots of shades and
widths. It can be bought at
hardware and electrical stores.

FINE PAINTBRUSH
You will need a clean, fine
paintbrush to write a message
in invisible ink.

IRON
Ask an adult to plug in and
use the iron. Even on a cool
temperature setting, an iron can
cause a serious burn, so better
safe than sorry!

KNIFE
To halve a lemon, you will need
a sharp knife. Ask an adult to
help you use the knife.

LEMON JUICER
This item is used to extract the
juice from lemons and other
citrus fruits. To use, press a
halved lemon onto the ridged
dome, press down and then
twist the lemon back and forth.
The juice will collect in the
bottom of the bowl.

NEEDLE AND THREAD
Plain thread and a needle are
all that you need. Try to match
the shade of the thread to the
shade of the felt.

PAPER GLUE
This is available in stick form
or in squeezable containers.
You can use white or craft glue
instead of paper glue.

PAPER TOWELS
You will need these to wipe
your hands and to clean
surfaces after completing
a project.

PENCIL SHARPENER
All you need is an ordinary
pencil sharpener.

Knife   Spoon   Scissors

Lemon juicer

Safety pins

RUBBER BANDS
These come in lots of sizes.
You can buy packages of rubber
bands at stationery stores and
supermarkets.

SAFETY PINS
For the projects in this book,
use medium or large safety
pins. Take care when opening a
safety pin – the pin may spring
out from the catch.

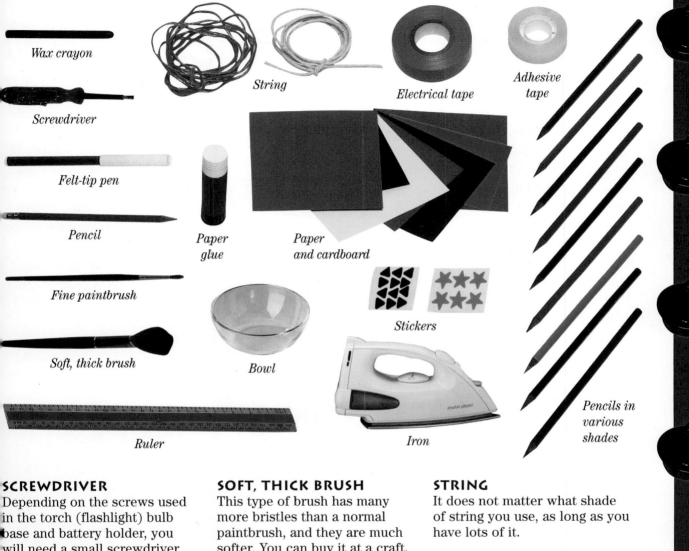

Wax crayon

Screwdriver

Felt-tip pen

Pencil

Fine paintbrush

Soft, thick brush

Ruler

String

Electrical tape

Adhesive tape

Paper glue

Paper and cardboard

Stickers

Bowl

Iron

Pencils in various shades

SCREWDRIVER
Depending on the screws used in the torch (flashlight) bulb base and battery holder, you will need a small screwdriver with either a straight or a Phillips head. Be careful when using a screwdriver, as the head of it has a sharp edge. Always use a screwdriver with an insulated handle.

SOFT, THICK BRUSH
This type of brush has many more bristles than a normal paintbrush, and they are much softer. You can buy it at a craft, stationery or hardware store.

STICKERS
Buy sheets of stickers at toy stores or stationery shops. You can use stickers in plain shades or shiny metallic ones.

STRING
It does not matter what shade of string you use, as long as you have lots of it.

WAX CRAYON
A wax crayon is perfect for shading large areas without making any impressions, or dents, in the paper. Choose a strong, bright shade for the project in this book.

Detective's Office

When a detective is not on surveillance or gathering evidence, he or she is in the office. It is here that the detective plans strategies for solving mysteries, makes specialized equipment and stores vital pieces of evidence. To fulfil these needs the detective's office must be well equipped and, most important, secure. (You do not want any old Tom, Dick or Harriet rifling through top secret documents, do you?)

Here is a list of must-have office items – a notebook for recording information, separate files for different cases and lots of pencils and pens.

You will need a telephone so that clients can contact you about jobs. A telephone will also save you lots of tiring legwork. Some detectives are on the telephone so much that it becomes stuck to their ears. To have it removed, he or she has to be disconnected. Ouch!

Do not use the telephone all the time – your family will not appreciate it. It is a good idea (and shows that you are a courteous detective) to ask for permission before using the telephone.

Detective's Kit

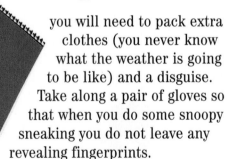

So that you are always prepared for an urgent job, have all your basic detective equipment packed in a sturdy backpack.

The basic kit consists of notebook, pencil, magnifying glass, plastic bags for storing physical evidence (for example, an empty food wrapper that may be covered with fingerprints), disposable plastic gloves for handling evidence, adhesive labels for identifying evidence and a camera or camera phone. For special jobs you may also need a torch (flashlight) and a pocket mirror.

For cases that will require long periods of surveillance you will need to pack extra clothes (you never know what the weather is going to be like) and a disguise.

Take along a pair of gloves so that when you do some snoopy sneaking you do not leave any revealing fingerprints.

Other items that may come in handy include money, maps and food. You must, of course, always carry your badge and ID card.

Before going on a case tell an adult where you will be. Detectives usually work in pairs or small teams (it makes surveillance jobs much easier), so also let the adult know who you are working with.

All About Disguise

A detective has to be a master of the quick disguise and costume change. But how do you do it without carrying around a suitcaseful of outfits? Easy – all you need is a change of clothes, a few simple props and a little bit of acting ability. Read on to see how it is done!

To change from streetwise detective to high-powered executive, wear a shirt and tie under your coat or sweater. Put a pair of glasses in a pocket and put a jacket, briefcase and mobile phone (a toy one will do) in your backpack. To make the transformation, whip off your sweater, don the jacket and glasses and hide your backpack in the briefcase. Now act the part by pretending to talk on the phone.

Useful items to collect for your disguise kit are hats, glasses and scarves (use these to conceal the lower half of your face). If you are working on a case where secrecy is paramount, buy a beard or wig at a costume or toy store. They are inexpensive and will fool everyone – even your family!

Surveillance Skills

Watching a suspect or a particular place for a long period of time without being detected takes a lot of skill. There are two ways of maintaining your cover – you either take cover and hide, or you blend in so that you are not even noticed.

If there is something for you to hide behind, use it. It does not matter what it is – a wooden fence, trees, a mailbox or a crowd of people – as long as you can easily see your suspect and he or she cannot see you.

Blending in with your surroundings is a bit more difficult. This is where disguises and simple props come in handy. In a shopping mall, surround yourself with shopping bags (looks natural) and pretend to study a shopping list. If your suspect is in a park, blend in by reading a newspaper or book and listening to music.

If you hold the newspaper or book up to your face it will protect your identity.

Now for the hardest job – watching someone in your own home. Brothers and sisters go bananas if you even so much as look at them, so the best cover is under a bed, in a closet or behind a large piece of furniture.

If you have to be a Super Sleuth in home territory, do it bearing in mind that you may not win any popularity contests. Always be considerate and never invade anyone's privacy – it could cost you your detective's badge and ID card!

Badge and ID Card

Making a detective's badge and ID card is your first assignment, Super Sleuth. Always keep them with you so that you can gain access to places that are off-limits to others. To make them look official, give yourself a James Bond-type code number and write it on the badge and card.

YOU WILL NEED

Cardboard
Scissors
Stickers or pencils, in various shades
Adhesive tape

Safety pin
Paper glue
Passport-size photograph of yourself
Felt-tip pen
Clear adhesive plastic

1 **To make the badge** – Cut a 6cm/2⅓in-wide circle from cardboard. If you want to, you can make your badge triangular, rectangular or even octagonal – any shape, as long as it looks official!

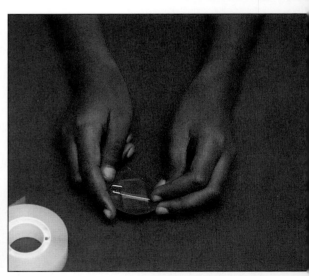

2 Decorate the front of the badge with stickers, or draw your own design using pencils. Use two or three pieces of tape to attach the safety pin carefully to the back of the badge.

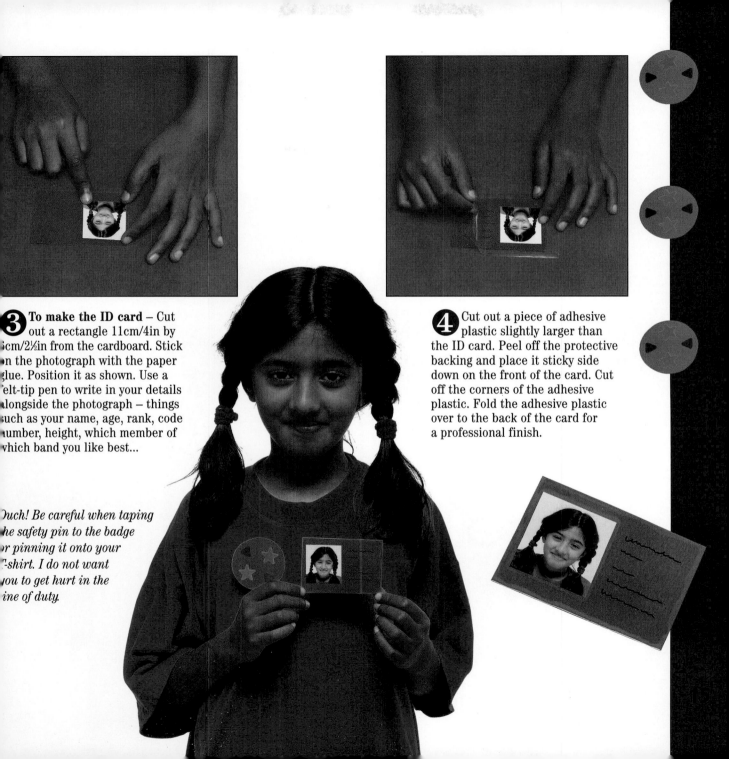

3 **To make the ID card** – Cut out a rectangle 11cm/4in by 6cm/2½in from the cardboard. Stick on the photograph with the paper glue. Position it as shown. Use a felt-tip pen to write in your details alongside the photograph – things such as your name, age, rank, code number, height, which member of which band you like best...

Ouch! Be careful when taping the safety pin to the badge or pinning it onto your T-shirt. I do not want you to get hurt in the line of duty.

4 Cut out a piece of adhesive plastic slightly larger than the ID card. Peel off the protective backing and place it sticky side down on the front of the card. Cut off the corners of the adhesive plastic. Fold the adhesive plastic over to the back of the card for a professional finish.

Dusting for Fingerprints

Everyone has a different fingerprint – it is as unique as you are! All the budding detective has to do is match the fingerprint found at the scene of the crime to one in his or her files. When an identical print is found, Super Sleuth will know the name of the culprit. Getting good, clear prints takes lots of practice, so leave no surface undusted!

YOU WILL NEED
Mug
Talcum powder
Soft brush
Wide, clear adhesive tape
Black cardboard
Magnifying glass
Pencil

1 Wash and dry the mug. This will remove any existing fingerprints. Then, without touching it with your hands, ask a friend to hold the mug firmly and then lay it on a table. Sprinkle talcum powder over the mug until it is well covered.

2 Use the soft brush to gently brush away most of the talcum powder on the mug. Do not blow on the mug – the moisture in your breath will cause the talcum powder to stick even where there are no fingerprints.

3 Keep gently brushing until you find a fingerprint covered with a fine layer of talcum powder. Brush around the fingerprint to remove any excess talcum powder. Handle the mug carefully so that you do not smudge the fingerprint.

4 To make a permanent record of the fingerprint for your evidence files, press a piece of tape onto the fingerprint. When you peel off the tape, the fingerprint will come with it. Sneaky and clever at the same time!

5 Stick the piece of tape onto black cardboard. The white fingerprint will show clearly against the black so that you can examine it under a magnifying glass. Write the name of the fingerprinted person on the back of the cardboard.

HANDY HINT
The best places to dust for fingerprints are on and around door handles, tabletops, stair railings and the handles of cups and mugs. It is much easier to get a clear and complete fingerprint from a smooth surface.

17

Taking Fingerprints

To take your own fingerprints, you must first find your fingers. Then you must be prepared to get them dirty! Once you have mastered the art of taking your own prints, build up a file of your family and friends' fingerprints. For each set of fingerprints, you will need cutouts of a right and a left hand stuck to cardboard. Do not forget to label the fingerprints with the name of the suspect.

YOU WILL NEED

Sheets of cardboard, in white and
*   other shades*
Pencil
Scissors
Paper glue
Ink pad
Paper towels

1 Place one hand on a sheet of cardboard and draw around it with the pencil. Repeat for the other hand using cardboard in a different shade. Your hands should be flat against the cardboard, fingers spread.

2 Cut out the templates of your hands. Use the paper glue to stick them, as shown, onto a sheet of white cardboard. Leave enough space above the fingers so that there is room to make the fingerprints.

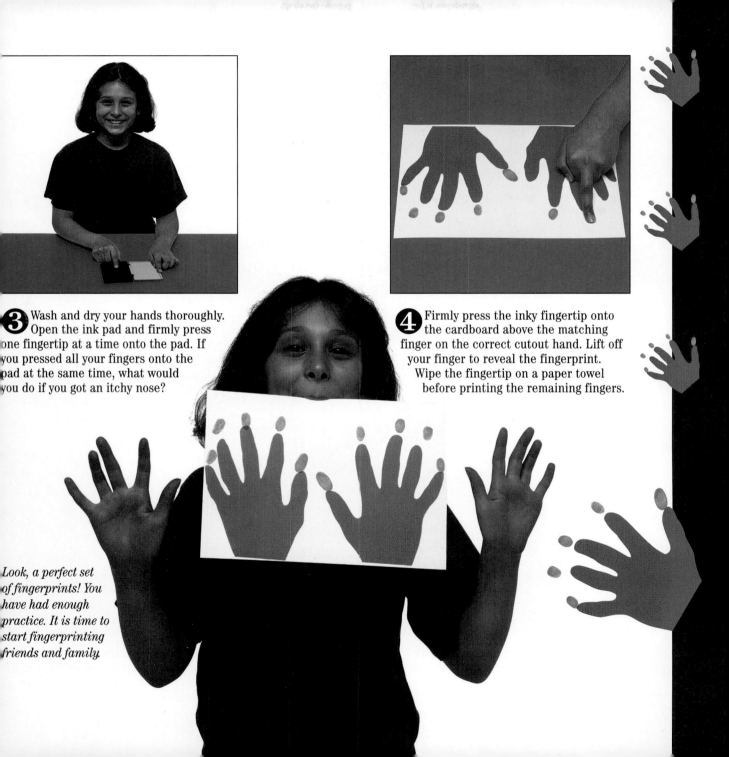

3 Wash and dry your hands thoroughly. Open the ink pad and firmly press one fingertip at a time onto the pad. If you pressed all your fingers onto the pad at the same time, what would you do if you got an itchy nose?

4 Firmly press the inky fingertip onto the cardboard above the matching finger on the correct cutout hand. Lift off your finger to reveal the fingerprint. Wipe the fingertip on a paper towel before printing the remaining fingers.

Look, a perfect set of fingerprints! You have had enough practice. It is time to start fingerprinting friends and family.

Seeing the Unseen

What should a detective do when a piece of written information is whisked away before his or her very eyes? The detective has to get sneaky! Here are two techniques for seeing the unseen – reading messages that you were never intended to read. Carry out the instructions to the letter and the message writer will never realize what you have done – unless you spill the beans!

YOU WILL NEED
Notepad
Wax crayon
Carbon paper
Scissors

1 It is easy to find out what someone has written on a page of a notepad and then torn out. The most important thing is to get your hands on the notepad – and be quick about it.

2 Use the crayon to gently shade in the top page. The small impressions made by the writing will remain unshaded. This technique will not work if the writing tool was a felt-tip pen or fountain pen.

3 To intercept a message, trim a sheet of carbon paper so that it is smaller than a page of the notepad. Turn over two pages of the notepad and insert the carbon paper, inky side down. Now all you have to do is wait!

4 Once the message has been written and the person is out of sight, turn the top pages of the notepad over and remove the carbon paper. On the page below is a copy of the message.

There is one other way of reading something that is not intended for your eyes – you could take a crafty look over the writer's shoulder. But be warned, you will be in grave danger if caught in the act. You may have to write off your career in the detective business!

Taking a Plaster Cast

The villain has left no fingerprints, but he or she has left handprints in the sand. The only way to record this vital piece of evidence is to take a plaster cast. It is a messy job, but someone has to do it. This project will help you get in some off-the-case plaster-casting practice.

YOU WILL NEED

Sand (moist sand works best)
Sheet of cardboard
Scissors
Adhesive tape
Mixing bowl

Plaster of Paris powder
Jug (pitcher) of water
Spoon
Large, soft paintbrush

1 Spread out the sand a little and gently flatten the surface. Firmly press one hand, fingers spread, into the sand. When you have made a clear impression, remove your hand. (No, not from your arm, from the sand.)

2 Cut the cardboard to make a strip 70cm/25 inches long by 8cm/2½ inches wide. Attach the ends with tape to form a ring. Apply more tape to seal the seam. Place the ring around the handprint and push it a little way into the sand.

3 To make the plaster of Paris, follow the instructions on the packaging. You will need to have a mixing bowl, a jug of water and a spoon ready. To make a good plaster of Paris mixture, keep stirring and work quickly.

4 When the mixture reaches a smooth, creamy consistency, pour it over the handprint. Use the spoon to ease the mixture gently into all the nooks and crannies. Pour on some more mixture to cover the sand evenly. To give the plaster cast a neat finish, spread the mixture so that it butts against the ring.

Most plaster of Paris mixtures take five to ten minutes to set, but this varies according to the thickness of the casting. When the plaster is hard, remove the ring and lift off the casting of your hand. Brush off any loose sand with a large, soft paintbrush. Only one thing left to do – clean up the mess!

Sneaky Book

The Sneaky Book lets you watch someone or something without being detected. Lots of tiny holes in the front cover and a hidden window in the back cover of your book let you see everything that is happening. No one will suspect a thing! The Sneaky Book also comes in handy when you want to watch television but are supposed to be doing your homework.

YOU WILL NEED
Sheet of cardboard
Scissors
Adhesive tape
Sheet of paper
Safety pin
Pencil
Ruler

1 Cut the cardboard to the same size as an open book. Fold in half. Tape one edge of the sheet of paper along the fold. Trim the paper to fit. Use the safety pin to make lots of holes in the front cover of your fake book, about 5cm/2in from the top.

2 Hold the fake book up to your face with the holes in line with your eyes. Pretend to be reading. What you are really doing is keeping a close watch on your prime suspect while keeping your identity safe. He or she will not notice the tiny holes in the book's cover.

3 Turn over the sheet of paper to reveal the inside back cover of your peekaboo book. Draw a rectangle 5cm/2in by 2.5cm/1in about 7cm/3in down from the top edge. Cut out the rectangle.

4 Cut out another rectangle, slightly larger than the window in your book, from a piece of cardboard of the same shade. Place this over the window and tape the top edge to the book. The flap should lift up easily.

5 To get a clearer view of your suspect, all you have to do is turn over the sheet of paper and lift up the flap. The open window can be easily spotted, so take a fast peek and then quickly close the flap.

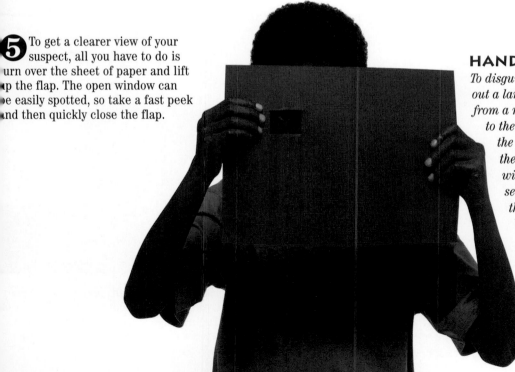

HANDY HINT

To disguise the window, cut out a large picture of a face from a magazine. Glue it to the back cover so that the position of one of the eyes is over the window. Cut out this section and glue it to the back of the flap. When the flap is down, the picture of the face is complete. When the flap is raised, your eye completes the picture!

25

Powerful Periscope

Powerful Periscope enables a Super Sleuth to look over tall fences and into high windows without climbing a ladder or scaling a tree. It will even let Super Sleuth see around corners. What makes it work? Mirrors, of course! The best mirrors to use are set inside a plastic frame and have a plastic backing. Never use your periscope to look at the sun; it will damage your eyes.

YOU WILL NEED
Large sheet of cardboard
2 mirrors, each 10cm/4in by 6.5cm/2½in
Pencil
Ruler
Scissors
Electrical tape
Paper glue

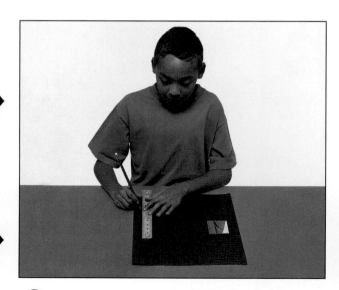

❶ Use the ruler to measure the width of the mirrors. Then draw five columns, each 40cm/16in long, down the length of the sheet of cardboard. Each column should be a little wider than the mirrors. Cut off any excess cardboard. Number the columns one to five.

❷ Draw a square near the top of side two. The square will be narrower than the width of the column. Cut out the square. Do the same at the bottom of side four. One window lets you look into the periscope, the other lets you see what is happening.

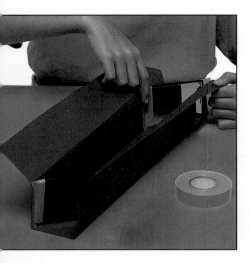

3 Crease the cardboard along each pencil line. Place one mirror, mirror side down, so that it covers the window in side two. Tape it in place along the top edge. Place the other mirror, mirror side down, to cover the window in side four. Tape it in place along the bottom edge. Now it gets tricky! Tape the bottom edge of the side two mirror to side four. The mirror will be angled to face down. Repeat for the other mirror, taping it to side two.

5 To use the periscope, simply place one eye against the bottom window. The top mirror will reflect whatever is in view to the mirror at the bottom.

4 Make sure mirrors are securely taped into position before closing the tube by folding side five over side one. Glue side five in place. Secure the seam with tape. Your periscope is now ready for action!

HANDY HINT
Getting the mirrors at the right angle so that your periscope works is tricky. It may be necessary to adjust the length of the tube and the size of the windows in sides two and four.

27

Mystifying Map

The Mystifying Map is one of my top detective tricks. It is easy to make, and only those who know the secret folding technique will be able to make sense of the map. Enemies who try to follow its false directions will end up going around in circles. Chuckle, chuckle! Draw a map that shows the way to a friend's house or to a secret meeting place and letter drop.

YOU WILL NEED
Sheet of paper
Pencils, in various shades

1 Fold the sheet of paper twice, as shown. The bottom flap is larger than the top two flaps.

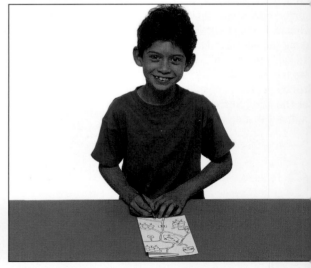

2 Keep the paper folded while you draw your map. Don't worry: the map is meant to run over the fold.

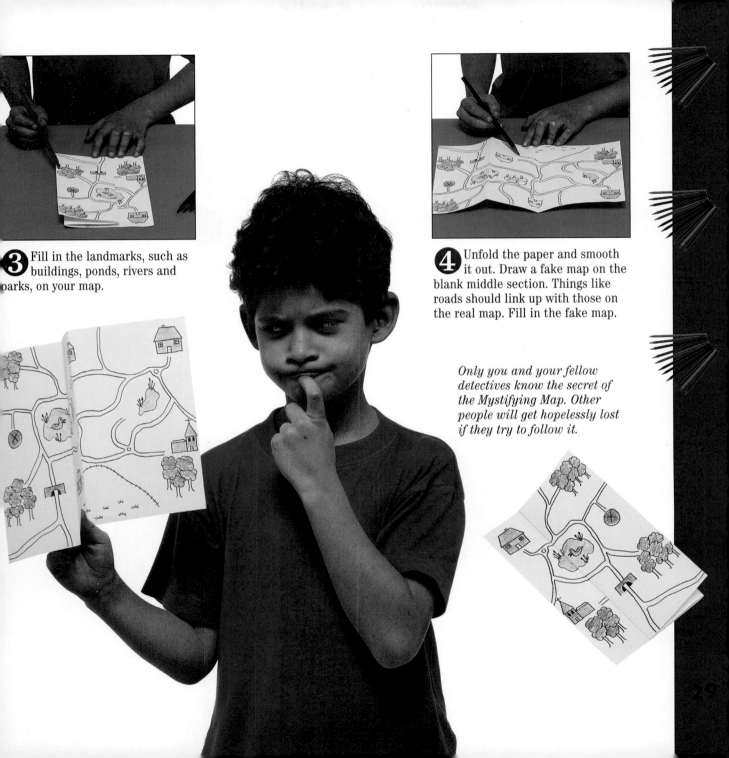

3 Fill in the landmarks, such as buildings, ponds, rivers and parks, on your map.

4 Unfold the paper and smooth it out. Draw a fake map on the blank middle section. Things like roads should link up with those on the real map. Fill in the fake map.

Only you and your fellow detectives know the secret of the Mystifying Map. Other people will get hopelessly lost if they try to follow it.

Hidden Camera

Okay, Super Sleuth, time to get some photographs of your suspects. It is crucial, of course, that they not catch you doing it. What you need is a Hidden Camera that is cleverly concealed inside an ordinary brown package. Are you ready for your latest assignment?

YOU WILL NEED

Pocket or disposable camera
Cardboard box, slightly
  larger than the camera
Pencil

Scissors
Electrical tape
Brown wrapping paper
Adhesive tape
String

1 Unfold the box with the inside facing up. Place the camera, lens down, on one of the sides of the box. Position it so that the shutter release button is close to one of the ends of the box. Without moving the camera, trace around the lens. Cut out this circle.

2 Put the camera back into its original position in the box, checking that the lens is in line behind the cutout circle. Use electrical tape to hold the camera firmly in position. Run tape both across and down the camera. Do not tape over the shutter release button.

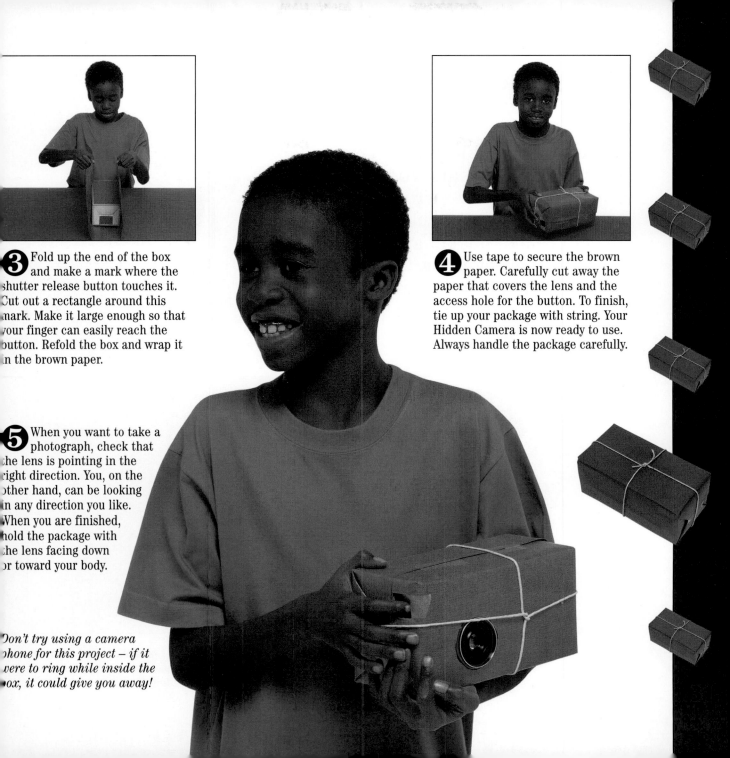

3 Fold up the end of the box and make a mark where the shutter release button touches it. Cut out a rectangle around this mark. Make it large enough so that your finger can easily reach the button. Refold the box and wrap it in the brown paper.

4 Use tape to secure the brown paper. Carefully cut away the paper that covers the lens and the access hole for the button. To finish, tie up your package with string. Your Hidden Camera is now ready to use. Always handle the package carefully.

5 When you want to take a photograph, check that the lens is pointing in the right direction. You, on the other hand, can be looking in any direction you like. When you are finished, hold the package with the lens facing down or toward your body.

Don't try using a camera phone for this project – if it were to ring while inside the box, it could give you away!

Secret Pocket

Detectives and spies often have to carry top secret documents. To prevent them from falling into the wrong hands if searched, ace agents hide the documents in a concealed pocket attached to the inside of their clothing. The Secret Pocket is easy to make and even easier to attach to a T-shirt. Just watch out for those safety pins!

YOU WILL NEED
Felt
Scissors
Needle
Thread
2 safety pins
T-shirt

1 Cut out a rectangular piece of felt 25cm/11in by 13cm/5in. You can cut out a smaller rectangle if you only want to hide small items. To make the pocket less noticeable, match the shade of the felt to your T-shirt.

2 Fold the felt in half to make a square. Thread the needle with the thread and tie a knot in the end. Sew up both sides of the felt to make a pocket. Do not sew across the top.

3 Attach the safety pins to one layer of felt near the opening of the pocket. Be careful not to prick yourself when securing the safety pins – those pins are sharp. Ouch!

4 Turn the T-shirt inside out. Make sure that you know which is the front. Open the safety pins and use them to attach the pocket to the inside front of the T-shirt. If you pin the pocket to the outside of the T-shirt, it will not be a secret!

Quickly conceal the precious document in the Secret Pocket while no one is looking. Try not to hide bulky documents in the secret pocket – it will give the game away. Before putting the T-shirt in the wash, do not forget to take out the hidden object from the pocket.

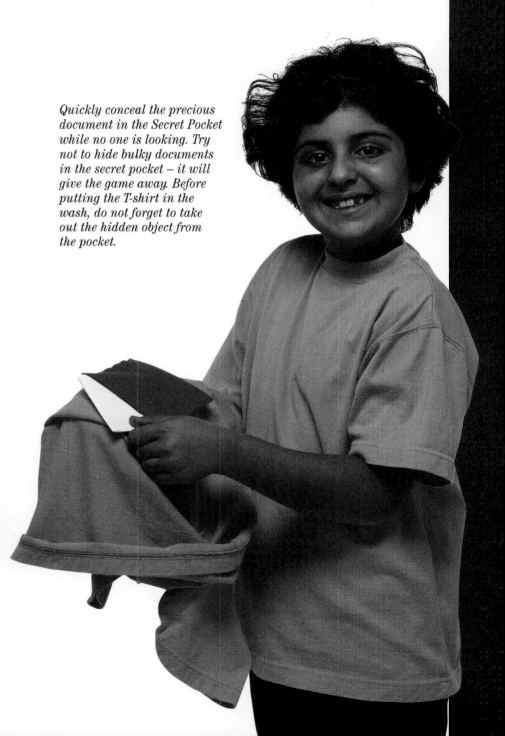

Detective's Wallet

Open one flap of this wallet and it is empty. Open it the other way and – wow! – there is the secret document. Make two identical Detective's Wallets so that you and a fellow detective can switch wallets (and secret information) without being detected. When using the wallet to trick someone, distract his or her attention so that he or she does not notice you turning the wallet over.

YOU WILL NEED
Sheet of cardboard
Pencil
Ruler
Scissors
Electrical tape
Piece of cardboard of a different shade

1 Draw three rectangles, each 20cm/8in by 8cm/3in onto the cardboard. Cut out the rectangles. You can make a miniature pocket-size version of this wallet by simply cutting out three smaller rectangles.

2 Lay the rectangles side by side and attach the edges with electrical tape, as shown. The tape should act like a hinge, allowing each piece of cardboard to fold over. Tape the seams on the back of the cardboard as well.

3 Attach electrical tape along the remaining two short sides. Position it so that it can be folded over to the back. Trim any excess.

4 Accordion-fold the wallet, as shown. Lay the wallet on the table and gently press it flat.

6 Turn the wallet over again and open the flap. If all has gone according to plan, the flap will contain the piece of cardboard. When turning the wallet over, do it discreetly, so nobody catches on to the trick.

5 To test your Detective's Wallet, place a small rectangle of a different shade of cardboard between two of the flaps. Close the flaps. Turn the wallet over and open the flap. If the flap is empty, you are doing it right. Close this flap.

Double Envelope Trick

To send top secret documents by mail, all good detectives use the Double Envelope Trick. This sneaky envelope has a hidden compartment that only fellow detectives will know about. Anyone else opening the envelope will find it empty. You can, if you want to, make up a false message and put it into the envelope to fool enemy agents.

YOU WILL NEED
Two large identical envelopes
Scissors
Secret message
Paper glue

1 Cut the front, including the flap, from one envelope. Trim a little off the edges of the cut section of envelope.

2 Slide the cut section of envelope inside the other envelope. The flaps on both should line up. So far, so good!

3 Place the secret message in the envelope, sliding it into the opening between the two flaps. Have you ever seen anything so sneaky?

4 Glue the two flaps together with paper glue. This will seal up the hidden compartment that contains the message.

5 If the envelope falls into the wrong hands and is opened, it will look empty. Your enemy will be very disappointed!

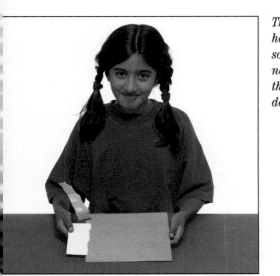

The envelope must have contained some surprising news, judging by the look on this detective's face.

6 You and your friends know exactly what to do with the Secret Envelope. Simply lift up the glued flap and rip it off. Slide a hand inside the now-open compartment and pull out the top secret message.

Undercover Book

You will have fun with this part of your detective kit – it fools everyone! To make the Undercover Book takes a little bit of time and lots of patience, especially if you want to hollow out a fairly deep hole. But I can assure you it is worth the effort. If you cannot find a large, unwanted book at home, you can buy one very cheaply at a secondhand bookstore.

YOU WILL NEED
Unwanted thick hardcover book
Pencil
Ruler
Scissors

1 Open the book at the front and turn over twenty pages. If it is a very thick book you can turn over more pages. Draw a rectangle on the right-hand page, leaving a 2.5cm/1in space to the edges of the page.

2 Use the scissors to cut out the rectangle. Using the hole as a stencil, draw the rectangle on the next right-hand page. Cut out this rectangle. Keep going until the hole is the right depth for the item you want to hide.

3 Do not cut into all the pages in the book – leave some at the back intact. Your hard work has paid off – your secret hiding place is ready.

4 Place your secret item inside the hollow and close the book. Put the Undercover Book on a shelf along with real books. No one will be able to tell the difference.

The Undercover Book can be used to hide all sorts of things, such as a tape recording of a secret conversation. (Of course, if the recording is on a CD then you could hide that in most books!) You can also use the Undercover Book to conceal snacks, money, a code book, a diary, or even a bicycle. (Well, maybe not a big bicycle!)

Delicious Disguise

Everyone has heard about sending messages in bottles, but only Super Sleuths know how to pass on vital pieces of information inside confectionery wrappers. There is only one problem with Delicious Disguise – resisting the temptation to eat the special treat! If you eat it and discard the wrapper, your message will be lost forever. Now, you don't want that to happen, do you?

YOU WILL NEED
Sheet of paper
Scissors
Pencil or pen
Confectionery in wrappers
Adhesive tape
Paper bag

1 Cut out a small rectangle of paper. Use this to write your secret message on.

2 Unwrap one piece of confectionery and place your message inside the wrapper.

3 Place the confectionery on top of the message and the wrapper. Rewrap the confectionery.

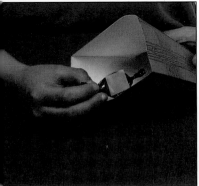

4 Make a loop from a short length of tape. The sticky surface should be on the outside of the loop. Stick the loop to the confectionery and then press that to the inside of the bag. Position the confectionery about halfway down.

5 Put the rest of the confectionery in the bag. Your secret message is now safe. No one will suspect that you are carrying vital information inside a bag of confectionery.

6 To pass on the secret message to a friend, all you have to do is empty the bag.

See, your secret message is safe! It is still stuck to the inside of the bag. Offer this to your friend. He or she can eat it while reading your note. Do not forget – as if you would – to take a treat for yourself!

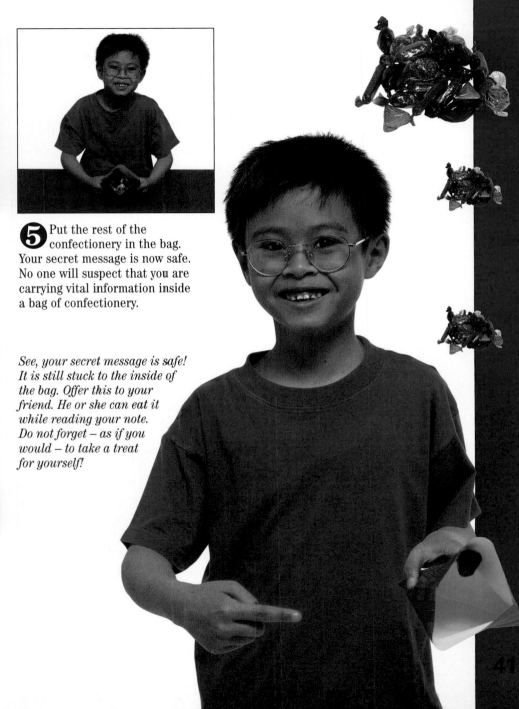

Handy Signals

Getting messages to other detectives can be tricky when you are involved in a hush-hush surveillance operation. So instead of shouting messages, use hand signals. On the next page are examples of just a handful (ha, ha!) of hand signals and their meanings. Use them alone to convey a simple message or link them together for more complicated instructions. When you have mastered these signals, go on to invent your own.

YOU WILL NEED

Your hands (preferably still attached to your arms!)

1 Press a finger to your lips when you want someone to stop talking. Move the finger over to your ear to say "listen".

4 Running a hand through your hair from the front to the back means "come here".

2 Resting your chin on a hand with the thumb pointing up means "yes". To say "no", point the thumb down.

5 Hiding your face behind one hand means "go away". Use two hands to say "go away quickly".

3 Place a hand loosely around your throat to warn fellow detectives that the situation is dangerous and to take care.

6 Placing a finger next to the right eye means "look right" and next to the left eye, "look left".

43

Flashing Messages

How can you send confidential messages over a long distance or at night? It is easy when you know how. All you need is a pocket mirror and a light. Before you and other detectives go on a mission, however, you will have to agree what each particular combination of flashes means. It might be a good idea to write the meanings and the secret signals in a code book.

YOU WILL NEED
Torch (flashlight)
Pocket mirror

1 A mirror is a great device for sending daytime signals. Hold it so that it catches the sun's rays, then jiggle it to flash a message.

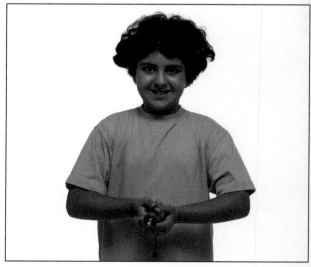

2 Torches are useful things. Without them you would just stumble around – oops, ouch! – in the dark. Detectives also use them to pinpoint their location.

3 Use the beam of light to spotlight a piece of evidence or a secret meeting place. To direct other detectives to a new position, move the beam from left to right or right to left.

4 By covering and uncovering the beam of light, detectives can send messages to each other at night. Use one flash to signal "all clear" and three flashes for "danger". Use special combinations of long and short flashes so that detectives can identify themselves or send more complicated messages.

Who is hiding in the bushes? Is she friend or foe? To find out, you will have to watch carefully as she flashes her secret code name.

Mirror Vision

To be a successful detective you have to learn all the tricks of the trade. The most important trick is knowing how to spy on people without being caught. This is where a small pocket mirror comes in handy. Simply tape it to a notebook so that you can see what is going on behind you. But be warned, you might find out something totally shocking!

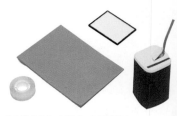

YOU WILL NEED
Spiral-bound notebook
Pocket mirror
Adhesive tape
Drink carton and straw

1 Tape the mirror to the front of the notebook. To hide the mirror from prying eyes, flip the back cover of the notebook over to the front.

2 Hold the notebook as if you are reading something written on the page. Angle it so that you can see what is going on behind you.

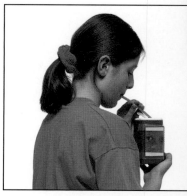

3 The mirror can also be taped to a drink carton. Angle the mirror so that it catches the scene behind you.

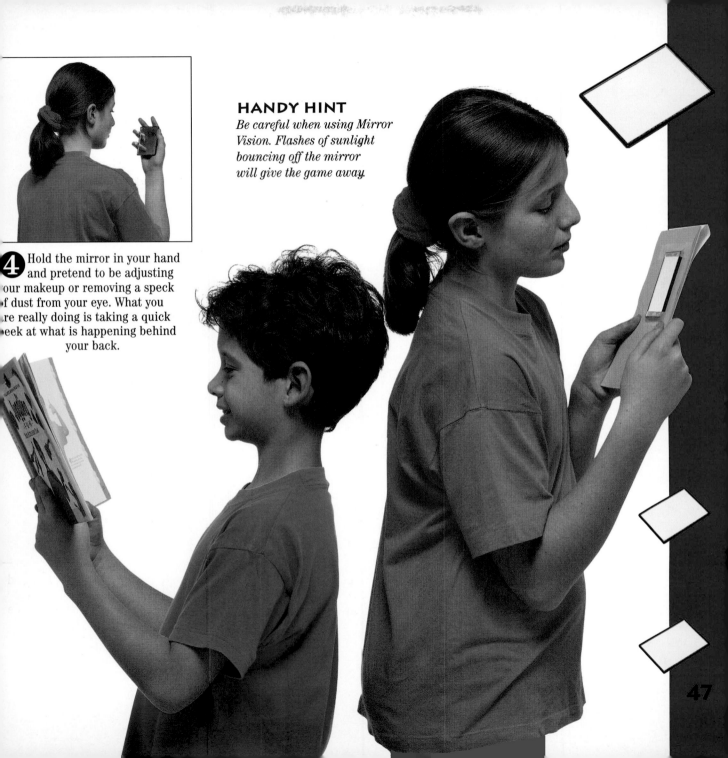

4 Hold the mirror in your hand and pretend to be adjusting your makeup or removing a speck of dust from your eye. What you are really doing is taking a quick peek at what is happening behind your back.

47

Invisible Writing

If you have never heard about Invisible Writing, then prepare to be astounded by this piece of detective trickery. To write an invisible message, all you need is a lemon, a fine paintbrush and a sheet of white paper. To read the message you will need to ask an adult to run a cool iron over the back of the piece of paper.

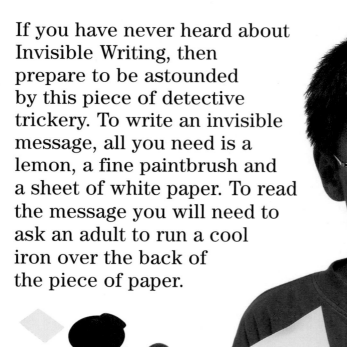

YOU WILL NEED

Knife
Lemon
Lemon juicer
Fine paintbrush
Sheet of white paper
Iron

1 Ask an adult to cut the lemon in half. Place one half on the lemon juicer. Push and turn the lemon to release the juice. Repeat with the other half.

2 Dip the fine brush into the lemon juice and write a coded message on the sheet of white paper. Let the paper dry before putting it in an envelope.

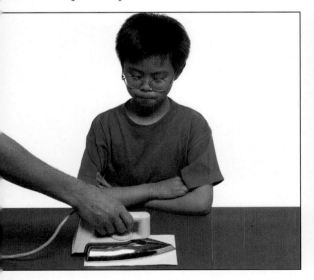

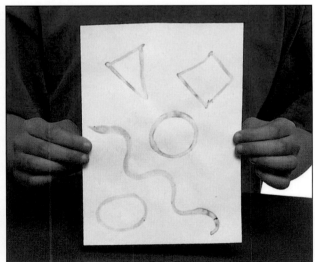

3 Now this is when the magic happens! To read the secret message, your friend must ask an adult to iron the back of the sheet of paper. The iron should be set on its coolest temperature.

4 When your friend turns over the sheet of ironed paper, he or she will be able to see the message. The heat from the iron has made the lemon juice turn light brown. Very clever!

Intruder Detectors

A Super Sleuth is highly suspicious of everyone – especially members of his or her own family, who may snoop around the detective's bedroom or office uninvited. To know when an intruder has been around, here are two clever Intruder Detectors for you to make. They are easy to install and completely sneakproof. These traps can also be set on closet doors, windows and drawers.

YOU WILL NEED

Scissors
Clear adhesive tape
Piece of cardboard

1 **Intruder detector number one** – use this door trap when dealing with a very clever and observant character. Even if the intruder suspects a trap, he or she will not spot this one. Cut a piece of clear tape 10cm/3½in long.

2 Position the tape so that one half is stuck to the door and the other half stuck to the door frame. Place the tape as close to the bottom of the door and frame as possible. When the door is opened the tape will become unstuck.

3 **Intruder detector number two** – not as sneaky as the tape trap but just as effective. Cut out a small rectangular piece of cardboard and fold it in half lengthwise. It is best to use cardboard that is a similar shade to the door that is to be booby-trapped

50

4 Insert the folded cardboard between the door and the door frame. Place it a little way up from the floor. Make sure the cardboard is firmly wedged. It should only fall out when the door is opened. If the cardboard keeps slipping out, it might be best to use Intruder Detector number one.

5 The trap has been sprung and the cardboard has fallen out! You now know for certain that someone has been in your bedroom. What is your next move, Super Sleuth? To hunt down the intruder or to set another trap?

Tricky Finger Pencil

All detectives need a Tricky Finger Pencil in their bag of tricks. This neat little device lets you record notes about your suspect while you appear to be innocently reading a book. The final sneaky touch is to make the cover of your notebook look like a book jacket. The book would, of course, be a detective mystery!

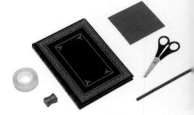

YOU WILL NEED
Pencil
Pencil sharpener
Piece of cardboard
Scissors
Adhesive tape
Notebook

❶ To make a Tricky Finger Pencil, you need a pencil 4cm/1½in long. You can sharpen one for hours to make it smaller or you can ask an adult to snap the end off a pencil. Sharpen the pencil to give it a fine point.

❷ Cut the cardboard to make a strip 7cm/2½in long and 2cm/1in wide. Wrap it around the top section of your thumb. Adjust the cardboard to fit and secure the seam with tape.

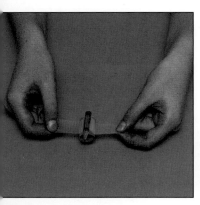

3 Place the pencil on the loop, as shown, and tape it into position. Make sure the pencil is attached securely so that it does not move around when you are writing. Your secret pencil is ready.

4 Place the loop of cardboard over your thumb. Turn the loop until the pencil is in the right position for writing. Make sure you are wearing the Tricky Finger Pencil on the correct hand! Hold the notebook in both hands, as shown, and try out using the pencil.

The Tricky Finger Pencil makes it easy to take notes about the suspect, without him or her suspecting a thing!

53

Electrical Trap

Making the Electrical Trap requires a little bit of technical know-how and patience. You might even want to ask an adult to help you with some of the hard parts. All your efforts will be worth it when the light flashes to warn you of an unwanted guest.

YOU WILL NEED

Piece of cardboard
Scissors
Aluminium foil
Adhesive tape
Small screwdriver

Plastic-covered copper
  wire, in 2 shades
Small torch (flashlight)
  bulb with base
2 batteries with holder

1 Cut out a strip of cardboard 15cm/6½in by 10cm/4in. Then cut out two squares of foil and tape them onto the cardboard, as shown. Fold the cardboard in half but do not let the foil squares touch each other.

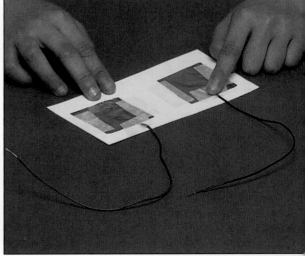

2 Ask an adult to cut two pieces of wire to the right length and to strip the plastic covering off the ends. You will need lots of wire if the trap and bulb are far apart. Tape a wire to each square of foil, as shown.

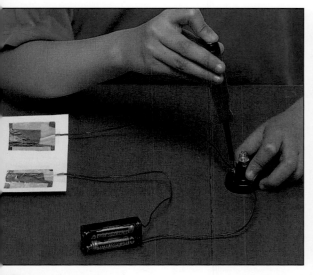

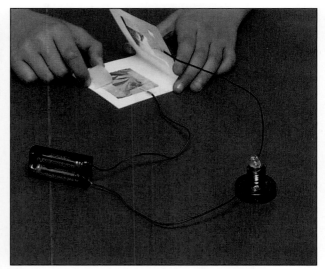

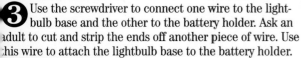

3 Use the screwdriver to connect one wire to the lightbulb base and the other to the battery holder. Ask an adult to cut and strip the ends off another piece of wire. Use this wire to attach the lightbulb base to the battery holder.

4 Make a loop of tape with the sticky surface on the outside. Stick this along one of the short sides of the cardboard. When someone walks on your trap, this loop of tape ensures that the foil squares remain in contact, thereby completing the electrical circuit. When the squares of foil touch each other, the lightbulb will go on!

5 Time to put your electrical wizardry to the test! Carefully place the folded cardboard under a rug. Make sure the foil squares are not touching. Position the lightbulb and batteries. Try to conceal the wires as much as possible. Press your foot down on the trap to make the foil squares touch. Bingo, it works! The light is on. Congratulations!

Noisy Alarms

Crunch, crackle, pop, squeak! What are those noises? They are the sounds of your latest security devices going noisily into action. I bet the intruder got a surprise!

YOU WILL NEED
Crunchy cereal
2 plastic squeakers

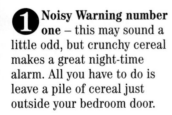

1 **Noisy Warning number one** – this may sound a little odd, but crunchy cereal makes a great night-time alarm. All you have to do is leave a pile of cereal just outside your bedroom door.

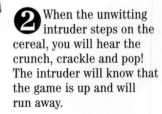

2 When the unwitting intruder steps on the cereal, you will hear the crunch, crackle and pop! The intruder will know that the game is up and will run away.

❸ **Noisy Warning number two** – place one or two squeakers under a rug. When someone steps on the squeakers, you will be the only one laughing.

❹ In case the intruder misses the squeakers under the rug, place another one under the cushion on a chair. Here are some other good places to hide squeakers – inside a shoe, in the back pocket of a pair of jeans and under the bottom sheet on a bed.

❺ When you hear the squeaker you will know that you have caught not a mouse, but a sneaky rat!

Spotting an Impostor

You are going to meet someone that you have never seen before. You have no idea what he or she looks like, as there are no photographs in the files. How will you recognize the agent? How will you know that the person you meet is not an impostor? Easy – use one of these spy identity card ideas. They are quick to prepare and totally spy-proof!

YOU WILL NEED
1 picture postcard
2 decks of playing cards

1 **Secret Signal number one –** tear the postcard in half and mail one half to the person you are going to meet.

2 When you meet, you both show your halves of the card. If the other person's card does not match, he or she is an impostor.

3 **Secret Signal number two –** telephone the person and agree to bring identical playing cards to the meeting.

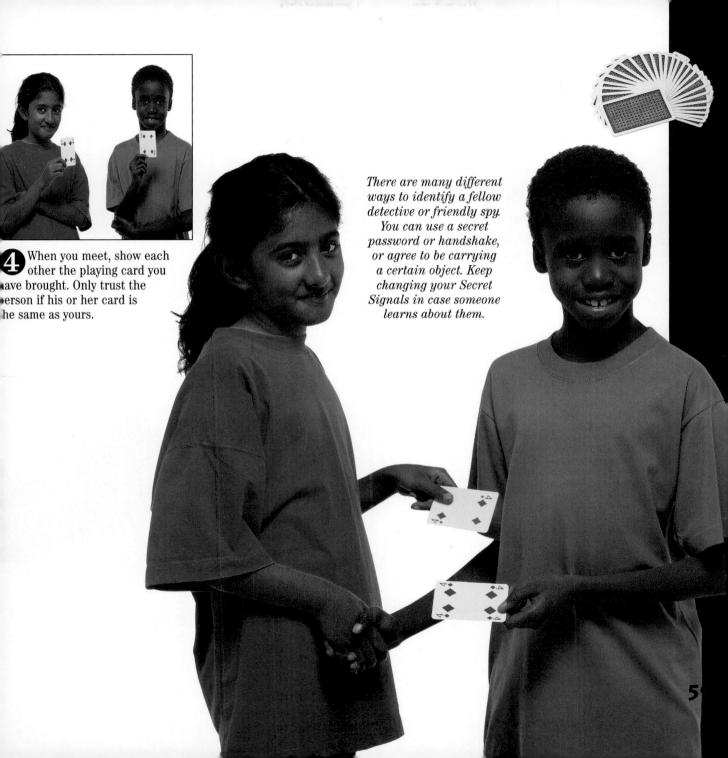

4 When you meet, show each other the playing card you have brought. Only trust the person if his or her card is the same as yours.

There are many different ways to identify a fellow detective or friendly spy. You can use a secret password or handshake, or agree to be carrying a certain object. Keep changing your Secret Signals in case someone learns about them.

Eye Spy

A detective has to use his or her powers of observation and deduction to solve a mystery. From a tangle of clues a detective must be able to find the right solution. To find out just how good a detective you are, try this Eye Spy game. To identify the objects you will have to look closely at the photographs and decipher the clues. Good luck, Super Sleuth! (Answers on page 64.)

YOU WILL NEED
Yourself
Your mind

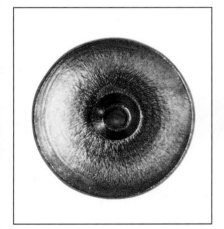

1 This item is very small and hangs around walls. Do you get my point?

2 This is a spicy one that may grind you down. Not a chance in a *mill*ion you will guess right.

3 To identify this one you will have to brush up on your observational skills.

4 These are bright objects that certainly leave their mark. This clue is too easy!

5 There is a children's song that fits this short and stout object down to a "T".

6 This item is useless when empty but refreshing when full. Boy, this game is thirsty work!

7 When you put something in this object, it gets bigger and positively blooms.

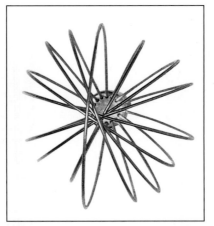

8 It takes a lot of huff and puff to make this object work. But when it works, it is very noisy.

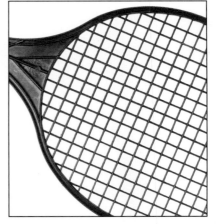

9 This item doesn't make a sound, yet it sounds very noisy. What could it be?

Final Challenge

The Final Challenge is the ultimate test of skill and daring for Super Sleuths. Your mission – if you accept it – is to retrieve the bowling pin from the circle using only string and a rubber band. You and your accomplice cannot enter the circle or touch the pin with any part of your bodies. The only part of the floor the pin can touch is the area on which it is standing. Good luck!

YOU WILL NEED
Chalk
Plastic bowling pin
Balls of string
Scissors
Rubber band

1 Draw a circle 1.5m/1yd in diameter using the chalk. (We have used a hoop in these photographs for clarity.) Place the bowling pin in the middle of the circle. Now, put on your thinking caps!

2 Cut four lengths of string 2m/1½yd long. Thread the lengths of string through the rubber band. The rubber band should be midway along each string. Hold the ends of the strings as shown.

Congratulations! You have done it! Now see if your friends can meet the Final Challenge.

3 Pull on the strings to stretch the rubber band so that it will fit over the top of the bowling pin. Lower the rubber band carefully over the pin.

4 Let the rubber band tighten around the bowling pin by relaxing your pull on the strings. Carefully raise the pin out of the circle. Do not pull on the strings, as this will loosen the rubber band's grip on the pin.

ACKNOWLEDGEMENTS

The publishers would like to thank the following children for appearing in this book:

Rula Awad
Steve Jason Aristizabal
Nadia el-Ayadi
Nicola Game
Kevin Lake
Isaac John Lewis
Laura Harris-Stewart
Pedro Henrique Queiroz
Jamie Rosso
Nida Sayeed

Gratitude also to their parents and to the Hampden Gurney School.

Nick Huckleberry Beak would like to thank John Freeman for keeping him sane (not that you would notice it, though) during the photo shoot. He would also like to thank his dad, and Barbara and Mike for helping with the ideas.

Nick Huckleberry Beak can be contacted at http://www.circustakeaway.co.uk/

Answers to Eye Spy (no cheating):
1. Spotlight lightbulb
2. Pepper mill
3. Hairbrush
4. Highlighter pens
5. Teapot
6. Mug
7. Flowerpot
8. Balloon whisk (half a point if you said a Dalek's gun!)
9. Tennis racquet